BOOK BENCHERS PUBLICATIONS PRESENTS

हस्ते ज़ख्म

{HASTE ZAKHM}

COMPILED BY –

AAYUSHI KHEDIA

AELAY PUBLICATION

A dream come true for every writers out there. We spot every possible problem for the writers, help in rectifying them and guide them towards the best outcome. We make sure to understand your needs, dreams and expectations, and nourish them with our services and stop not until we fulfill your dreams. The writers have a right and freedom to choose what they want here. They have us to guide them through the hardest path until the end. Believe in us.

Aelay Publication - by a writer for the writers.

BOOK BENCHERS

Book Benchers is the affiliate of Aelay publication. Both the publication is handled by Astro.
Aelay plays the role of publishing solo books.
And Book Benchers is epically for publishing anthologies.

Book Benchers have 2 different teams.
1. Tamil

2. English/Hindi

Never mind what our main motive is to help all the budding writers, who are seeking for their dream of publishing their own book to come true.

We are there to help out everyone.
In guiding for starting up with your carrier in compiling until finishing up your full book.

Book Benchers

<u>COPYRIGHT</u>

(Affiliate by Aelay Publish)

Book: Haste zakhm
Compiler: AAYUSHI KHEDIA
First Edition: Augest 2021

Published By:
The Book Benchers
5/175, Fathima nagar,
Kuthenkuly,
Tirunelveli -627104
Phone: 9944992571

Design And Executed by

ISBN : 978-93-5533-182-3
Page : 113

ACKNOWLEDGEMENT

"Haste zakhm" will define the pain behind a fake smile, the sufferings in ones life. The one who hides billions of throbbings to make someone happy. Acknowledgement is essential to boost up passion, making person more valid and precious, giving the team a great progress that makes worth.
We would like to use this opportunity to thank each and every one who all the people involved in this book and, more specifically, to all the co - authors .Without your support, this book would not have become a reality. We would like to thank each one of the authors for their contributions.
Our sincere gratitude to all who contributed their time and expertise to this book. We wish to acknowledge the valuable contributions of the Publication regarding the improvement of quality, coherence, and content.
Last but not least, we would like to extend our gratitude to parents and friends who have been a huge support through the book.

DISCLAIMER

" **HASTE ZAKHM** " under **Book Benchers Publication House** is a work of fiction. All the thoughts, writings has been penned by the imaginative purpose of the writers itself. We do not take any responsibilities in case of plagiarism of content found as the publication, founders nor the compilers would be responsible for this. The writers will be the sole source of the above same.

<u>FOUNDER</u>

IRUDAGA ASTRO

Irudaga Astro, From Tirunelveli, Founder of
Aelay and BB (Book Benchers)
He had completed his BE.
He has written 3 Tamil poetry book's which
hits the top list on social media!
His main aim is to allow the writers to
publish their words as their book rather than
just Posting them on Insta.

LINK AND POSTER MAKER

CATHERINE ASMI T

Catherine Asmi T, From Tirunelveli
She has completed her M.com
Her passion is Drawing and Designing.

<u>TEAM HEAD</u>

She is a passionate writer from Chennai. Writing makes her pressure go away. She had played the role of co-author for more than 100+ Antho's. She would like to thank her parents and her Loveable Brother for supporting her rather than stopping her from what she wanted to do! For being the main reason for achieving her dreams. As well as for standing beside her in all the ups and downs. Whenever she feels like she needs to get out of her stressful timing or feels like she needs peacefulness, she starts to paint, she would never mind sitting in the same place for so many hours when it comes to her painting. She believes that anyone could hurt her, But never her books could!!

Catch her in Insta and FB
Insta: @theinnocentheart
FB: KA. PARINASRI

CONTENT

1. Prashant Bhardwaj
2. anushree mondal
3. vineet kumar
4. tanzeela ilyas
5. catherine sheena
6. Deepanshi gupta
7. shaswat Sourav sahoo
8. Har Deepansh Bahadur Sinha
9. Anushree Alva
10. Ravi Shrivastava
11. Lipsa Dabhi
12. Aradhana Damani
13. Jasmine Panda
14. Swayamshree Chakravarty
15. Shivam rai
16. Tarini Prasad Mohapatra
17. Amit kumar
18. kumari radha
19. arjun singh kashyap
20. Juli Jaiswal
21. Shivang Sharma
22. Aswin S A
23. Kajal bhargav
24. Anuradha Gupta
25. Md. Junaid Mondal
26. Naveen bhardwaj
27. Fareeha Faiyyaz
28. Srishti Morya
29. Rajan Vishwakarma
30. Rachna mehra

31. Vaishnawi Kumari
32. Sristy Saha
33. Ankita Nahar
34.Shubham
35.अनूप सिंह जोनवाल (गुमनाम शायर)
36. Sahil Lamba
37.Gita kumara
38.Mohit Singh Rajput
39.Sudiksha Kshatriya
40.Saloni Gupta
41.Silachi Kumar " Vयोgi "
42.ANKIT CHAHAL (Do_lafj 📖📖)
43.Trapti Gupta
44.Pathan Fatima B .Alam
45.Tannu Kumari
46.Pankaj THAKUR KP SHAYAR
47.Abhishek mehra
48.Disha gupta
49.Adam Joseph abram
50. Kavya Mittal

AAYUSHI KHEDIA

Aayushi Khedia is a seventeen yr old girl belonging to Purulia , West Bengal . She is a budding writer who likes to express through words , convey her feelings through pen. Influenced by her own life she started writing at the age of 9 yrs and has a habbit to pen down her thoughts ad feelings in her writings. She is a girl with thousands of dreams , on her way to achieve those.

She believes in – "words speak louder than actions"

Insta : dazzing_aayu

Stolen_soul

Email id : aayushikhedia11@gmail.com

HASTE ZAKHM

दर्द भरी मुस्कान

....

हर मुस्कान के पीछे एक कहानी होती है,
छुपी लाखो परेशानी होती है।

कुछ को खुश देखने के खातिर हस लेते है कभी ,
छुपाने की कोशिश करते है अपने दर्द सभी ।

तकलीफ में भी चेहरे पर मुस्कान रहती है,
जो बैयां न होकर सब सहती है ।

बड़ी रहस्यमयी होती है उनकी जिंदगी ,
करते है वो कितने बंदगी ।

यह दर्द नहीं समझता है कोई ,
नहीं देख पाते जो खुशियां है खोई।

दर्द का एक अलग ही रिश्ता है ,
जो रोकर भी हसे वो फरिश्ता है ।।

....

© Aayushi khedia 🖤

PRASHANT BHARDWAJ

Co-author Prashant Bhardwaj is a student from Palamu, Daltonganj . He believes sometimes words speak. Through his shayerisss, he tries to express his feelings which he can't speak. He is not a writer by profession but writing is his passion. He wrote his first shayari for her girlfriend to annoy her. He always write for her to let her know his feelings. His writings touches the heart of the readers.

Insta id : unkahibaatein_0112

HASTE ZAKHM

इश्क कभी ना करना मोहब्बत हो जाएगी,
जिसकी दीदार करने की चाहत हो वो कहीं गुम हो जाएगी.
जनाब इश्क बहोत जालिम चीज है,
आपको छोड़ किसी और के बाहों में सो जाएगी।।।

....

दिल हमारी नाजुक है बहुत,,
यू तोड़ के ना जाइए।।

छोड़ कर जाइए,,
मगर यू दिल तोड़ के ना जाइए...

कमजोर हूं मैं बहोत,,
मेरी दिल के जैसा..

छोड़ कर जाइए,,
मगर यूं दिल तोड़ के ना जाइए।।

Anushree Mondal

I'm Anushree Mondal of 11th from west bengal and residential in odisha parents: punlin mondal , mukul rani Mondal Love to dance classical and passion is writing poetry .... Love the family most.
Insta id : @Charming_Sathi24

HASTE ZAKHM

I wanted to... love waited ❣
 I want you to remember
But time changed me
It was good for both That we separated
 If you have no time For me
 No care for me
 So why?
You came in my life Now why?
 You are ignoring me But! He is not person of your
Loveable soul
It's a person of just a showing layer!!
 By telling me no time I wanted to remember those
day
My heart says noo
Love waited
 For a while But didn't regret we feel
 I never thought,he will wait So,love waited
 I think, love recognised my feel It filled my heart
with a Colourful roses, when he waited For while
 Told one think repeatedly
 That I have recognised you by my feel With a little
eagerly zeal...
 For a while Long time...
Love waited a while And regret I feel for my guilty
deal..

Vineet kumar

Vineet Kumar is pursuing MBBS studies and now he is a third year student, He is fond of writing, reading books , listening to songs, especially he is also a good chef , home baker. He started writings since his childhood when he was studying 5th standard he penned down his first note about his feelings , for him writing is all about emotion and part of his life, whatever he writes is what he feel and think about himself randomly and he need not to think too much to write about Something.

Insta id : Vineet1086

HASTE ZAKHM

दुनिया परेशान है

जहां देखो वहां कोरोना का ही नाम है

सारी दुनिया एक कमरे की गुलाम है

फिर भी सरहद पर सैनिक खड़े खुलेआम है

डॉक्टरो को सारी दुनिया की तरफ से सलाम है

इस संकट के समय में डॉक्टर ही भगवान है

इसे रोकना हर इंसान का काम है

एकता का बल दिखाओगे तो इस महामारी से
बचपाओगे

जात पात का राग गाओगे बेमौत मारे जाओगे

बेमौत मारे जाओगे.....

Tanzeela ilyas

Tanzeela ilyas from Srinagar Kashmir , India. she is 19 yrs old.she is Co author of some published books and is also co author of this book

Life

Life is the beautifull gift form almighty God;
No definite time may be short or long.

crammed with divergent colours we see;
Every colour has its own gravity.

The colours are so brightened;
Oh! we make it complicated.

Depends upon us how we use it;
Relevant is to compromise with it.

We imagine anything and happens something;
This is the process that we are performing

Catherine Sheena

Sheena Catherine is a girl with plenty of dreams.
She is a nineteen years old girl who is still trying to
achieve her dreams. Her pen name is
sheenacathrinebelle. She likes to write poems, short
stories, quotes etc. She is a broad minded person.
She believes that words speak greater than action so
she writes from her heart.
Insta id :- sheenacathrinebelle

HASTE ZAKHM

Alone.

Without you,
I feel like I'm drowning in a bottomless pit.
Hear my heartbeat is pounding,
By seeing my days without you,
I feel no shame in crying.
Whatever it takes ,
I just want to be with you.
Wondering how can I touch your heart,
On my way to destiny,
When I'm facing the reality,
I don't want be walking alone.
Even if I go astray in deepest maze,
Will this maze guides me to you.
Gentle wind, lonely breeze,
While missing you,
The cold wind tries to break us apart.
Even if I lost in despair,
Your warm breeze will comfort me ..
Words that were written down,
I erased them one by one and the last word
That remain is you !
I lost in your thoughts,
Now there is no way to sleep,
I can't bear the loneliness between us..
The stars were shining to me away,
Whispering I want you to know,
You're my world.
The scenery and weather are lovely,
Be close to me, my beloved...

Deepanshi gupta

Deepanshi gupta is of 21 years. Recently she completed her graduation. She is from saharanpur uttar pradesh. She is not a professional writer. Its her hobby. She want to do something great in this feild and want to achieve name with fame from this inspiring feild of writing. Good luck dear❤

HASTE ZAKHM

तेरी आंखो में आज ये मदहोशी कैसी?

तु सोया नहीं रात भर?

क्या बात हुई ऐसी?

इश्क, महोब्बत या प्यार तो वजह नहीं,

जानती हूं मैं की ये बेवजह नहीं,

ना इश्क है ना महोब्बत और ना ही है ये प्यार जाना,

इस मदहोशी की दोषी है जिम्मेदारियों का आजाना।।

-दिपांशी गुप्ता

Shaswat Sourav Sahoo

Shaswat Sourav Sahoo, is an eighteen-something adventurer who grew up traversing the wonders through the pages of metaphors. He fell in love with books and never reverted. Today he is pursuing his studies and living a clichéd life at NISER as an Integrated M.Sc. research scholar. He has been recently awarded with the Global Achiever's Award.

HASTE ZAKHM

She was the charm
He got into her arms
Huffing and puffing
Slowly and calm.

Dizzy became his eyes
Drizzle over his body
Laid the two bodies
Insouciant and transient

Teary eyed wailing was she
With wounded and bruised knee
He kept his head over her lap
But the god of jinx had the see.

"I love you" he gasped
She couldn't speak, sobbing
He smiled, things came to an halt
And the unspoken words she left
Could no longer keep her alive.

© Shaswat Sourav Sahoo

Har Deepansh Bahadur Sinha

He is Har Deepansh Bahadur Sinha . He belongs to Lucknow,UP. He has done masters in Geography from National Post Graduate College. Completed his schooling from Study Hall. His hobbies are art , listening to music , cooking & loads of driving. His interest areas are Astronomy, Writing, Photography & Travelling a lot.
Insta id :- Deepansh_sinha

HASTE ZAKHM

We Miss You

She was blessed with fabulous smile
Along with some phenomenal style,
She was the power house of positivity
Among our circle she was the celebrity.

For friends she did loads of sacrifices
She left us today it's tough to digest,
We genuinely lost a superstar
Now she has gone too far.

After her death everything got changed
Routine got disturbed which was arranged,
The grief which we cannot explain
Daily we went though unbearable pain.

We were so closely attached
From us she got snatched,
Who will understand our emotions
Numerous months ago we lost expressions.

We created her artificial presence
Life was tough in her absence,
Whenever we friends went for drive
But they were simple without surprise.

Anushree Alva

Co - author Aaina Alva, currently from Mangalore, Karnataka. She's pursuing BCA and never planned to be a writer but was definitely destined to be one. Her journey started from reading novels to collect qoutes and ended up writing qoutes on her own. Influenced by ups and downs of her own life, she started writing qoutes and wants to be read and relate by people.
Insta id :- aainas_diary

HASTE ZAKHM

After you left,
Did I realize your role in my life..
Now I've stopped blaming you because You
showed me that

I was worth much more..
Showed me that side of me
which I didn't know existed..
made me realize that I can be strong enough
by myself and get up right where I fell from
without waiting for someone
to grab my hand to pull me up..

■■■■■■■■■■■■■■■■■■■■■■■■■■■■■■■■■■■■■■■

The moon faints away
as the lustrous sun rises..
Yet we adore the moon though it has flaws..
You came into my life like a moon.. Spreading
brightness in my dark life
without burning me out.
. Though there are many sun's around me,
I still adore the moon like you..

Mr. Ravi

Ravi Shrivastava is from Motihari, East Champaran, Bihar. He is currently work in CSC e-gov. of india. He is a professional Business Man and writer.He goes by the pen name 'Mr. Ravi'. He is all types Quots, Poetry, Sayari and short-Story writer. His hobbies are travelling,photography and writing.He is first write co-author book on "Syahi"(स्याही) Publisher by Spring Buddies and second co-author book on "वक्त-ए-मुसाफिर" Publisher by Droplets of ink publication and co-author work in other books..

HASTE ZAKHM

इस दिल ने कितने ख्वाब सजाये थे
आँखों से होकर इस दिल में सामिल हुए थे
और चन्द अफवाहो ने क्या घेरा तुम्हें
बिच राह में ही यूं तन्हा मुझे छोड़ आये थे

प्यार की धूप धल गई

नजरे भी थक गई

तेरी राह तकते-तकते

लौट कर न आया वो हरजाई

कर गया मुझसे बेवफाई

दे गया मुझे तन्हाई

वर्दास्त न होती ये जुदाई

थक गए अब जिंदगी से

सोना चाहते जिंदगी भर के लिए

न जाने कब हमे ये मौत है आई

माथे पर तेरे नाम की बिन्दी लगाई है,
गालो पे लाली, होथो पे मुस्कान सजाई है,
अब तो आजा ओ परदेशी सजन,
अब ये जुदाई बर्खास्त न होती,
आज मुझे तेरी बहोत याद आई है,
By-RaVi (परदेशी सजन)

Lipsa Dabhi

She is lipsa dabhi. She is Author and also good Co-Author. She is eighteen years old, she is student of the computer engineering.She is extraordinary person. She is always good leader. Her mam mrunal prajapati is her inspiration person and also her motivater, her friend chetna raval also supported to her and her mom manisha ben and her father nilesh bhai also supported to her for anytype of her creativity. she also wrote poems, short stories,shayries. Her writing skills almost very well and her creative collections are always best
Insta id :- __lipsa__dabhi__0829

HASTE ZAKHM

एक तरफा छिपा हुआ प्यार

आज तक प्यार को मेरे एक तरफा रखा हैं मैं ने,
ना नाम दिया उसे कोई,
छिपा हुआ सा रखा प्यार मेरा,
इसीलिए कभी वो दो तरफा बना ही नहीं ।

प्यार को मेरे एक तरफा सा रहना पड़ा,
एक बार इजहार किया था उससे प्यार का वो तो मझाक
समझकर बैठा,
इस कदर प्यार एक तरफा रह गया ।

छूपा ना पाए तुझे कही ऐसा राझ हो तुम,
मेरे दिल में बसनेवाला पहला प्यार हो तुम,
हर कोई फिका लगता मुझे तेरे आगे,
ऐसे ही रह गया छिपा प्यार मेरा ।

Aradhana Damani

Hello, All the writings are from the core of my heart I feel very happy and relaxed when I convert my thoughts into poems .

Insta id :- @aradhanadamani

HASTE ZAKHM

Life and death

Death is unpredictable
Is life predictable
None of these are permanent
So control your temperament
Everyone of us are temporary
So why to worry each moment unnecessarily
Live life to its fullest
After death no one knows what's going to happen
next.

Jasmine Panda

Miss Jasmine Panda is presently pursuing Ph.D. Chemistry from Ravenshaw University, Odisha, India. She is a Gold Medalist and University Topper in her B.Sc. and M.Sc. Apart from being a versatile orator and debator, she has been a part of 480+ anthologies till now and loves to pen down her feelings! She has compiled an anthology "Vasudhaiva Kutumbakam" under SOI publication which is also the best seller#9. She is an amiable person interested in both Science and Literature, having a wide variety of interests like painting, sketching, acting, anchoring, debating, rangoli making, taking part in extempore, elocution and many more...Publishing her own book someday is something which she aspires.

HASTE ZAKHM

Question of Survival

Today question is raised on our survival,
We are fighting with a new invisible rival!
Today's time is giving us a secret message,
Seems like Nature is taking revenge!
But it's the only outcome of our activities,
Thinking it will open new possibilities!
But it only helped to create negativities,
Seems like humans have crossed all boundaries!
It's time to understand the secret message,
Meaningful message, Without much time wastage!
Everything will be alright very soon,
If we understand, our life is a boon!

By Jasmine Panda

Swayamshree Chakravarty

Swayamshree is a 12th grade student from Odisha.
Being a co-author in 75+ anthologies, she's also a
trained dancer and a guitarist. Her writings are
based on her past life and what she has
experienced!

OT7

HASTE ZAKHM

How devastated i was
When i didn't care much about myself
That's when the seven guys
Came up with love yourself
Yeah you got me right
I am talking about BTS
Whom else i can refer to
When my feelings completely changed, to be
honest
From hurt to heal
They motivated me with their songs
Whatever they do armies support them
We have bias, but we truly support OT7 🖤

Shivam rai

मै शिवम राय ग्राम पोस्ट रेवतीपुर जिला गाजीपुर उत्तर प्रदेश का रहने वाला हूं।मेरा जन्म 15 अगस्त 1997 को रेवतीपुर गांव में ही हुआ।हाईस्कूल और इंटरमीडिएट की पढ़ाई केंद्रीय स्कूल गाजीपुर से हुई है।स्नातक की पढ़ाई वीर बहादुर सिंह पूर्वांचल विश्वविद्यालय जौनपुर से हुई।इसके बाद मुझे नौकरी लॉजिस्टिक्स में मिल गई।अब मै एम बी ए की पढ़ाई ए के टी यू लखनऊ से चल रही है।मुझे अलग अलग प्रकार की किताबें पढ़ने और हर एक विषय पर बोलने और लिखने का शौक है!!

Insta id :- @shivam_rai_9896/
@shivam_rai_8892

"हसते जख्म"

जहाँ प्यार की एक सीमा हो वही सच्चा प्यार होता है, क्योकि प्यार भी जब हद पार कर जाती है तो....वह भी अभिशाप बन जाती है| जब दिल टूटता हैं ना दोस्त ! तो आवाज भी नही आती लेकिन पूरा शरीर सहम उठता हैं| दर्द भी होता हैं और दिखाई भी नही देती| तड़प भी होती हैं और मरहम भी कोई नही लगाता|

अगर आपकी आशिकी हद पार कर चुकी हैं फिर दर्द ही मिलेगा और अगर नही की हैं तो गलती कैसे भी हो, चाहे स्थिति कैसी भी हो सबसे पहले आप खुद एक बार माफ़ी मांगिये| गलती किसी की भी हो दोस्त ! जिम्मेदारी दोनों की हैं| उसके बाद भले ही कुछ पल के लिए शांत रहो|

एक बात याद रखियेगा अगर वो आपकी हैं तो मुश्किलें कैसे भी हो, हालात जैसे भी वो लौट के जरुर आएगी और आयेगी जरुर| अगर नही आती तो समझ लीजियेगा आप ने एकतरफा मोहब्बत कर ली हैं दोस्त ! जिसको आपके जज्बातों की कोई अहमियत नही हैं|

Tarini Prasad Mohapatra

My self Tarini Prasad Mohapatra from Odisha. My pen name is Naren and my passion is to write poems stories dramas Shayaris articles etc.

Insta id :- tarini.mohapatra.940

HASTE ZAKHM

Our desires are a home,
Painted with emotions .
Adorned with romantic ambience
And embellished with love experience.
Our desires are a home.
We are it's foundation.
This home brings the soul together, with feelings
and attraction.
The needs pleasure and satisfaction
All are the rooftop and the floor.
Your beauty and my expression,
Are it's door.
The windows are the expectations and
your and my communications,
Are it's artification.
This home of desire is the only thing which I need.
I need you in my home of desire,
And have no greed.

Amit Kumar

अमित कुमार बिहार के उभरते लेखकों में से एक है।जिन्हें कक्षा ७ से ही कविताओं से लगाव है इन्होंने अभी तक ३० से भी जायदा कविताएं लिखी है।फिलहाल अमित कुमार कर्नाटका में स्तिथ राष्ट्रीय मिलिट्री स्कूल, बेलगाम में अपनी पढ़ाई कर रहे हैं। आप इनकी कविता और कहानियां पढ़ सकते हो

इंस्टाग्राम-_perfect_mr_21

ईमेल- yadavamit4721@gmail.com

HASTE ZAKHM

मेरी मोहब्बत,

तु मुझसे क्यों रूठ जाती है,

तुझे तो मालूम है ना,

मनाना नहीं आता हमें,

तो फिर जरूरत में साथ क्यों छोड़ी जाती है,

तुझसे इश्क करने की इजाजत नहीं मांगता मैं,

पर मेरे इस पाक इश्क को तू फ़िज़ूल का नाम दे इसकी

इजाजत भी नहीं देता मैं।

आज यह लिखते हुए मेरी कलम थक सी गई है और मैं

थम सा गया हूं,

देख तो सही जो दर्द देकर गई है उसे बयां भी नहीं कर पा

रहा हूं।

आज तेरी नाराजगी को नजरअंदाज नहीं कर सकता मैं,

चल माना तुझे भुला नहीं सकता मैं,लेकिन सुन!

तुझसे दूर जाने के बाद तुझे अपना भी नहीं सकता मैं।

जा रही है ना मुझे छोड़कर तो जा,

पर एक एहसान करती जा,

इस दुनिया को हमारी मोहब्बत की झूठी दास्तान सुनाना

मत,

मुझसे दूर चले जाने के बाद झूठे आंसू बहाना मत,

एक अरसे बाद चैन की नींद सोने जा रहा हूं,

कब्र पर मेरी या मुझे जगाना मत।

Kumari Radha

राँची शहर में पली बढ़ी इस नवोदित रचनाकार का नाम राधा है।पर्यावरण , नारीवाद ,एवं अन्य सामाजिक विषयों पर लिखना इन्हें बेहद पसंद है जिनकी विधा कविताएं,शायरी एवं कहानियां के रूप में होती है। इनकी रचनाएं सह-लेखक के तौर पर 11 से अधिक संकलनों में प्रकाशित हो चुके हैं। लेखन के अलावा चित्रकारी, फोटोग्राफी एवं यात्रा करने में भी इनकी गहरी रुचि है।आप इनसे जुड़ने के लिए इनके instagram page को follow कर सकते हैं :-@lafz_e_dil__

क्या फ़र्क पड़ा?

HASTE ZAKHM

उन्होंने पूछा क्या फ़र्क़ पड़ा हमारे जाने से?

हमनें कहा ज्यादा कुछ नहीं-

पहले चेहरे पर मुस्कान ख़ुद ही आ जाती थी,
अब जब्र ही लानी पड़ती है...

पहले बेफिज़ूल सी बातें सुनने वाले तुम थे,
अब अपनी बातें चाँद-तारों को सुनानी पड़ती है..

. पहले गिरने पर तुम्हारा हाथ सामने पाते थे,
अब ख़ुद से ख़ुद को सँभालने की आदत पड़ चुकी है...

पहले ग़म में तुम्हारे कंधे पर अश्क़ बहाते थे,
अब इन सिरहाने पड़े तकियों को मेरा सहारा बनने की
अदा आ चुकी है...

©radha

Arjun Singh kashyap

हमारा नाम अर्जुन सिंह कश्यप है उत्तर प्रदेश के बरेली जिले के रहने वाले है हमने बरेली के जयनारायण इण्टर कॉलेज से इण्टर किया है। Mjpru रोहिलखंड से संबद्ध बरेली कॉलेज बरेली के छात्र है हम समय, सामाजिक जीवन, समाज, सच्चाई पर बेहद खूबसूरती से लिखना पसंद करते है, हमारी रचनाएं तेरा चेहरा, दिल के जज्बात, खामोशी, Aesthetic silence नामक पुस्तक में प्रकाशित हो चुकी है।

HASTE ZAKHM

शब्द क्या है?

युद्ध के मैदान में
वीर को वीरत्व की प्राप्ति कराये,
हां वही शब्द है।

उदास व्यक्ति को
मुस्कुराहट दिला दे,
हां वही शब्द है।

निर्बल, निसहाय व्यक्ति को
पुरजोर हौसला दे,
हां वही शब्द है।

प्राचीन नफरत के रिश्तों में
एक नई उमंग, उल्लास आ जाय,
हां वही शब्द है।

एक परिवार में
भातृत्व, मातृत्व, पितृत्व को जगा दे,
हां वही शब्द है।

Juli Jaiswal

नमस्कार.. मेरा नाम जुली जयसवाल है ।मैं मुज़फ्फरपुर बिहार से हूं। मुझें किताबें पढ़ना और कविता लिखना बहुत पसंद है । मैने सह लेखक के रूप में कई किताबों में कविता और कहानी लिखी हैं । उम्मीद करती हूं कि आप सभी को मेरी ये कविता पसंद आएगी ...धन्यवाद

Insta id:- @jyotsana61116

HASTE ZAKHM

सहमीं हुई फिजायें
डरी डरी हवाएं
सहमे हुये उजाले
बेबाक हैं अंधेरे
चारों तरफ हैं मेरे
उदासियों के घेरे
उदासियों में अपने
गुमसुम सी हो गई हूं

जीवन के इस सड़क पे
कितने है मोड़ आएं
उलझीं हुई हैं राहें
बुझी बुझी निगाहें
और शाम हो गई है
रास्ते में खो गई हूं

ज़ख्मी है सोच मेरी
अहसास में नमीं है
मैं खुद में ढूंढती हूं
मुझमें कहाँ कमीं है
वीरान ये आसमां
उदास ये जमीं है

Shivang Sharma

शिवांग शर्मा आज के युग के नए शायर हैं। शायर साहब वाराणसी के निकट स्थित मऊ जिले से आते हैं। इन्होंने कई पुस्तकों में सह - लेखक और संकलक के रूप में काम किया हैं। शायर साहब वर्तमान समय में राष्ट्रीय प्रौद्योगिकी संस्थान पटना से इंजीनियरिंग कर रहे हैं। इनके लिखने का सिलसिला क्यूँ शुरू हुआ ये आपको नीचे के लेख में दिखेगा - " मिलता नहीं मुझे कोई अकेला रहता हूँ मैं , लेता हूँ सहारा कलम का पन्नों पे चीख देता हूँ मैं। "

Insta id :- ___chailover___
___dil_e_alfaaz__

HASTE ZAKHM

शादी करेंगे हम

रहें सही सलामत तो
तुझसे शादी करेंगे हम,

देंगे तुझे हज़ार खुशियाँ
फिर माँग तेरी भरेंगे हम,

प्यार करते हैं हम तुझसे
ज़िस्म की वफ़ा नहीं,

झूठी बातें कर के
झासा नहीं देंगे हम,

हो तेरी हामी तो
तू भी कुबूल कह देना,

तेरी हामी होने तक
किसी को कुबूल नहीं कहेंगे हम।

Aswin S A

Aswin S.A. is a budding writer. He writes in various themes exploring the true meaning of existence, connecting literature with various aspects of love and life. He writes his poems with extreme passion and all his words are filled with rhyming vividness. There is so much to learn about life from his inspiring lines. I've known him personally and he is such a person with uniqueness as his lines. Do read the lines and enjoy for yourselves.

Insta: let_me_write_something__

HASTE ZAKHM

Wound is a Weapon

A Man with no wound
Is a Man with no sound.
In the entire world,
Wonded man burns like a fire
In the wild.
He is a restless tire
With the Mild.

Speaking less
Showing victory in action.
Setting goal
Working with an reaction.

But more cautious regarding
The words he use.
When it precautioned,
He cures the wounded.

Kajal bhargav

she is an aspiring writer hailing from Lucknow
Uttar Pradesh she is passionate in
writing,music,dance, Reading books. her dream is to
become professor and writer in future.
Insta id :- Kajal bhargav2897

HASTE ZAKHM

हाल–ए–जख्म...

हर हाल में मुस्कुराना हैआंसुओ को छिपाना है
तेरे लिए अपने दर्द और जख्मों को भुलाना है ।

तेरे प्यार की याद को अपने दिल में दफनाना है
सोचकर तेरी बातों को अब जीते चले जाना है ।

तेरी इन्ही बेरुखियों को अपना हौसला बनाना है
टूट कर हूं बिखरा पर फिर भी मुस्कुराना है ।

कतरा कतरा होकर भी बिना थके चले जाना है
जज्बातों से खेलने वालों को हाल न बताना है।

तेरे दिए जख्मों को देखकर भी हंसते रहना है
एक मोम की तरह जलकर पिघलते रहना है।

नासूर सी बातो को दिल से नही लगाना है
सब कुछ भुलाकर,जिंदगी से कुछ सीखना है।

मोहब्बत–ए–जख्म में मुझे ये उसूल बनाना है
कितना भी सह लेना पर दूसरो को न डूबना है।

एक सच्चा इंसान बनकर इससे निकलना है।
सताए जख्मों को भरने के लिए नही तरसना है

ANURADHA

Anurdha is 20years old female, Mumbai,
Maharashtra. She is completing her Graduation in
Bachelor of Accounting & Finance Degree.
Anuradha has been an active participant in Litrary
Arts, Fine Arts & Performing Arts Competitions
throughout her life. She is also a member of
NATIONAL SERVICE SCHEME in her college
and worked at district level activities of Social
Services. Her hobbies are Travelling, Photography
& Photoshoot.
Insta id :- rukmani0000official

HASTE ZAKHM

•MR. JOKER•

Life of a Joker,
Started from when he woke her...
The tears soaker,
And the heart broker...
Known as Popular Smoker,
From the day he choke her...
Inspite of making her laugh,
The loyalty & love he got half...
She treated him like happy staff,
Behind the false Photograph...
Hidding all the hostile,
He shows the world his Bold Smile...
Even after drinking pain's wine,
Acting like he's absolutely fine...
Deleting her thoughts line by line,
Moving towards darkness; still he shine...
Absorbing all the Pain,
Controlling the Brain...
Which has already gone insane,
Because of the Unexpected Rain...
Nothing left to explain, Nor to Maintain...
Removing all her stain,
He got connected in the affection Chain...
The memories which trouble again & again,
Now whom to approach for them to complain..

Md. Junaid Mondal

Md. Junaid Mondal is born and brought up in Kolkata. He is a student of standard 12. As it is a universal truth that poetry is the finer spirit of all living science. He believe that words have the power to transform. He had penned his first poem entitled "Mom and Dad" at the age of 14. Since then a sort of reality stamps deeply on his mind what Wordsworth said "poetry is the spontaneous overflow of mind" and indeed words came so gracefully and effortlessly that a book in 2019 "Read to Explore " published containing almost 50 poems.Insta id :- mjm03_official

Helpless

I am in pain mommy,
Things are changing daily,
I don't understand any,
My heart can't stand so many.

Dreams are shattering in front of me,
Where are my moments of glee?
People make fun of me,
May be I am funny but not free.

They are breaking every inch of mine,
There words are like bites of canine.
Day by day my pains are only intensifying,
Now my body don't get relieved even by
novocaine.

My heart is all damage,
Hopes are inside the cage.
This war no long I can wage,
The world inside is like swage.

Naveen bhardwaj

Myself Naveen bhardwaj a programmer by profession a lover of poetry maker and like reading books and audiobooks and he has telegram channel @TheNBbook
insta I'd na.vin7832

HASTE ZAKHM

One of the most precious and valuable things in
life when we can change the way we look at
ourselves ; when we go beyond the superfluous
our reality because it is very easy for us to acquire
the condition of more or less it is very easy for us
to judge our difficult , but it's reality that we value
and love ourselves .
Crowd will cheer for you as long as you can
entertained them . Money can buy you a luxurious
lifestyle; but after your death nothing matters ,
what the point of having all luxurious in the world
if you are not able to receive a proper funeral after
your death . Money can't buy you a true friends ,
love and eternal happiness.
The worst kind of boredom is not knowing what
you are tired of so you start deleting everything
that you think may have caused it ; but you see in
the end you left with nothing and you see you are
still alone and you are tired and there is nothing
something else , so you haven't to do everything
from the beginning as if .
Your good looks aren't enough to make a person
falls for you brings out your talent and abilities ;
because the person who falls for looks are always
temporary lovers . For permanent love your good
looks works as the icing on the cake but the real
flavour of a cake is decided by what type of
person you actually are don't be proud of your
looks you have got them in your genes , be proud
of your talent that's what you actually earn .

Fareeha Faiyyaz

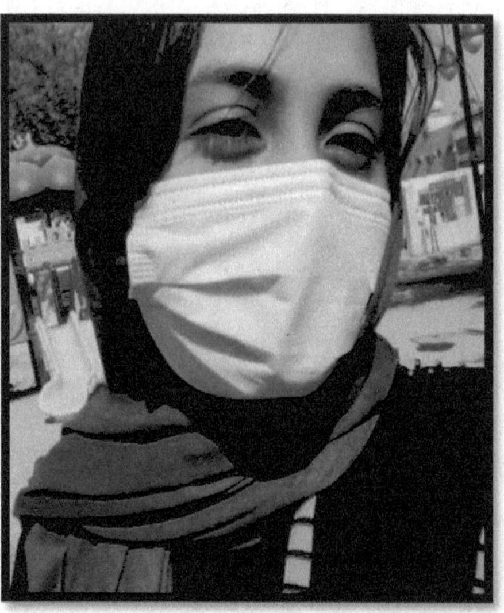

Fareeha Faiyyaz is a student and a writer who is deeply intrigued by the universe of emotions and feelings. Her writeups are reflection of her journey of self love. She is also a published co-author

Insta id :- charmingfrequencies

Rain

The patter unfolds
Sooths my ailing heart
Unable to Express
As skies pour and earth heals
My heart goes along with it
And heals my weary soul

Srishti Morya

Coauthor Srishti Morya is studying Journalism. She love to write down quote, poem, story and letter to editor.her letter to editor publish in a newspaper and also published poem in college magazine. She is a very creative girl and a imaginary girl which create a story in dream and write in a copy. She belongs to Faridabad Haryana.
Insta id :- 4526shiny

【 हँसी में भरे गहरे ज़ख्म 】

कुछ बोल न पाके भी में उसको,

देखकर उसे समझ जाया करता,

गहरे ज़ख्म जो चले है उसपे,

की वो दर्द भी हँसी में छुप न पाये,

बहुत कष्ट है राहों पर,

उसे सुलझाना बहुत है मुश्किल,

अंधेरो में भी छिपते कदम,

वो परछाई भी हमकों दिख न पाएं,

उस हसीन मुस्कान में न जाने,

कितने गम बसे है उसमें,

दिखाई न पड़ती उसकी खामोशी,

जब पर्दा करती अपने मुस्कान से,

दिल में इतने जख्म भरे,

की बयां भी किसी से हो न पाएं,

बस अपनी प्यारी मुस्कान को लेकर,

यूँ ही जीवन हमसफ़र बन जाए।

Rajan Vishwakarma

DOB 02 JUNE
Photography
Nature lover
Master of COMMERCE
Writing(not for passion)

Insta id :- @rajan.vishwakrma

HASTE ZAKHM

" शाम- ए - दास्तां "

बैठा था मै गुमसूम कही
घर के एक कोने के पास
सोच रहा था कुछ यूही कहीं
कि तभी आया सुमंतोष(Vयोगी)का फोन मेरे पास,
बोला वो की क्या आओगे तुम टहलने आज!
मैंने बोला हाँ आओ अभी आज चलते हैं
स्टेशन के पास,
निकले हम अपने घर से मिल के दोनो टहलने साथ,
कुछ वो बोला और कुछ मै बोला
और हो गयी शुरू कुछ अनसुने बात,
टहलते टहलते खत्म हुआ आज की ये बात,
कल फिर शुरू करेंगे कुछ नई चर्चा दूसरे के कहानी के
साथ,
चले हम अपने घर फिर करके महादेव के उदघोष के
साथ,
फिर कल मिलेंगे वही जहाँ मिलते थे रोज एक साथ।।

Rajan Vishwakarma " मनमौजी "

Rachna mehra

She is Rachna mehra a 19 yrs old business management student. She is from bihar. She is interested in writing or start writing before 7 months ago. She is also interested in traveling. You can search her on instagram as. s.o.u.l._.stealer.04

HASTE ZAKHM

कहते हैं जिंदगी बड़ी मुश्किल है,

ये सब लोग कहते हैं लेकिन महसूस सिर्फ मध्यम वर्गीय परिवार कर पति है,

जब जैसा वक्त आय वो कभी नहीं हार मानता है,

अपनी परिवार की खुशी के लिए अपने ही परिवार से दूर से होता हैं,

 लोग कहते हैं एक मध्यम वर्गीय परिवार का इंसान बचपन में ही जिम्मेदार हो जाता है जब उसे अपने जिम्मेदारी का एहसास होता है,

 वो पढ़ते हैं अपने सपने पूरे करने के लिए ऐसे तो कई लोग अपना सपना भूल जाते हैं,

 लेकिन जो लोग अपना सपना पूरा करते हैं,

कड़ी मेहनत से करते है,

 जिंदगी उन्हे कई मोड़ पे हरा देता है लेकिन वो फिर खड़े हो जाते हैं,

 चाहे परिस्थति जैसी भी हो वो कभी हार नहीं मानते है।

अपने दर्द भरे एहसास को पूरी दुनिया से छुपाते हैं,

इनके पास बड़ी मकान या लंबी गाड़ी न हो लेकिन वो जो हर गम भूला दे ऐसी मुस्कान होती है।

 मुझे गर्व है की मैं एक मध्यम वर्गीय परिवार से हूं मैंने देखा है अपने पापा को मेरी खुशी के लिए अपनी एक छोटी सी चाहत छुपाते हुए,

अब तो बस मेरा सपना यही है की मैं उनके सारे सपने पूरे करू।

जिन्होने मुझे नाम दिया मैं उनका नाम रोशन करू।

Vaishnawi Kumari

Vaishnawi Kumari is the co-author of 10+ world record anthologies along with 150+ successful creations with different publications. Her books have received praise and recognition from many well-known publications. This gorgeous poetess belongs to Patna, Bihar, and she is an upcoming computer science graduate from NSIT, Bihta, Patna. There are 4 upcoming projects as an author. She uses it to inspire and empower young people through it. You can personally contact with her Instagram handle @kumarivaishnawi and can follow @mystic.vaishu to see her amazing creations.

एक कफन चाहिए

अब ये जिंदगी कब्रिस्तान सी लगती है,
ऐसा लगता है मानो कितने ख्वाहिशों को अपने इस दिल में
दफना कर रखे हैं,
ना कोई सुनने वाला है ना कोई समझने वाला है,
यहां तो लोग अपनी राय देने वाले हैं,
जब जरूरत होती है हमारी तो लोग मदद मांगते हैं और
बदले में धोखा दे जाते हैं,
आ जाए कभी मुसीबत तो हमारा ध्यान आता है,
और अगर काम निकल जाते हीं "तुम कौन हो"
ऐसा कह कर नजरअंदाज़ कर जाते हैं,
सारी इच्छाएं खत्म हो चुकी है जिंदगी जीने की,
अब तो बस एक सुकून चाहिए,
हां! मुझे एक कफ़न चाहिए।।।।
ना अपनों ने साथ दिया ना मोहब्बत में हाथ थामा,
बस हमसे अपने हिस्से का प्यार लेते गए और बदले में
दगाबाजी देते गए,
शायद गलती मेरी है,
जो हद से ज्यादा मैंने प्यार और उम्मीद किया,
क्योंकि मैं तो भूल ही चुकी थी यह दुनिया ही मतलबी है,
अब बस इस रूह को सुकून चाहिए,
मिले जहां इस आत्मा को शांति वह जगह चाहिए,
हां! मुझे एक कफ़न चाहिए।।।

Sristy Saha

Hey there!! This is Sristy, a student of 11th
standard in Humanities who loves poetry, books
and music...nature heals her heart...

Insta id :- sristy___40

HASTE ZAKHM

A flowing river

I see the river flowing away, but the water I can't
utilise,
As I am dealing with the huge, robust walls of
despise....

As I think of getting released by completing the
last chore,
A powerful intruder arrives and binds me more....

The monsoon has filled this river upto its peak,
The only way of water inlet I continuously seek....

I am a thirsty prisoner who has received the sun's
strength not the warm glow, Who has watched the
different phases of this river through the prison's
window....

If I'm unable to use the water this time, it will be a
long, rough wait of a year again
Till which I know not whether I will sustain....

Being a stranger to all these facts, the river
continues to flow without getting its content
utilised,
The intruder arrives again - giving me more
reasons to get despised...

Sristy Saha

ANKITA NAHAR

#AKII#@@@
Ankita Nahar, physically she live in AJMER,
RAJASTHAN but heartly live in everywhere. She
is too much passionate about writing. She have
always found comfort in words, and thats what
attracts everyone. Writing is her therapy, she write
what she feels and experiences in her life. You
can take a look at her writings on Instagram
@naharankita1

HASTE ZAKHM

I have come ahead leaving everyone behind,
I was never so mean before.
As much as he wanted his own,
He inflicted the same pain on him.

The surprising thing in that too is this,
That all of them went so far after.
Like never before
Like you've never met before.

I still look back I want to go back
to those moments too.
But I'm not mean,
For the wounds that everyone inflicted on me.

©AKII#@@@

Shubham

s

I am Shubham from Hajipur. I am student of BBA. But my passion is to write poetry. I love to express my feelings through my poetry. If you want to read my more poetry do visit my Instagram page -- @alfaaz.

हँसी का सफर

ये खामोशी भी कुछ कहने लगी
बीते लम्हों की हर बात याद आने लगी है

खोया हुआ हूँ उन खयालो में
धूल पड़ी तेरी तस्वीर नजर आने लगी है

दिल का हाल ना पूछो खबर जैसे सुना तेरे जाने की,
सियाही-रात में चाँद की रौशनी सताने लगी है

जमाने के दिल मे हमदर्दी थी मेरे लिए
पर मैं खुश हूँ मेरे हिस्से में तेरी याद आने लगी है

ये हकीकत है तेरी यादों के साहारे जीना है
ये बात पहले रुलाती थी अब लबो पर हँसी देने लगी
है।।

Anoop Singh jonwal

में एक लेखक हूं
मुझे लिखने का बहुत शौक है
मेरा नाम अनूप सिंह जोनवाल है
में दौसा राजस्थान का निवासी हूं
Insta id :- @Bittu.anoop

HASTE ZAKHM

जब में दफ़न हो जाऊ तो मेरा इश्क़ मुकमल लिख देना
गर लगे तस्वीरें चौराहे पर मेरी तो
तस्वीरें के कोने में उसका नाम भी लिख देना

Sahil lamba

I'm sahil lamba. My age is 17 and I'm in 12 th class.

Insta id :- Sahil.__.025

Sometimes you have to smile
And move on,
Because no one cares.

Gita kumari

I am Gita from Chittaranjan West Bengal. I am a graduate Bba(hnrs) student and now pursuing for competitive exams . I love to read and write books .i worked as a co-author in many books ..though i believe that writing is a prefect way to talk without being interupted in someone's life.

Insta id :- Sonar7922

HASTE ZAKHM

2am

You and me ..
Under the sky..
Watching the stars..
With a cup of tea..
Lots of talks
And
Sharing some memories...

Mohit Singh Rajput

Myself Mohit Chouhan, I am graduated with B.A.
in English literature and i am a computer operator as
well. I started writing during lockdown, my main
motive behind writing is to spread possitivity and
make world peaceful. I love to write about life.....
Life is all about hope ❣

Insta id :- @_mohit_singhrajput_

मेरी प्यारी बहना...

अकेला चुना था क़िस्मत ने मुझे ज़िंदगी के सफ़र में,
पत्थर दिल सा बना दिया था हालातों के असर ने,
बस नफ़रत और अंधेरा भरा था दिल में मेरे,
मानो खुशियां भर आई महज़ तेरे आने के ज़िक्र से।

जैसा सोचा था वही बात दिखाई दी तुझमें,
अंधेरों में रोशनी सी बनकर आई मेरी ज़िंदगी में,
आने से तेरे मैने जाना प्यार के असल मायने,
वरना हमेशा से बस खोया रहता था खुद में।

बेफिक्र हुआ करता था कभी दिल बरसो से,
कुछ बदला सा लग रहा है कल परसों से,
अब तो फिक्र खुद से ज्यादा है मेरी प्यारी बहना,
दिल सहम सा जाता है तुझे खोने के डर से।

तुझे ज़रा सी तकलीफ हो तो देखा नहीं जाता है,
तू परेशान हो किसी बात से तो कुछ समझ नहीं आता है,
दूर होकर भी तुझसे बेटू मुझे एहसास हो जाता है,
तुझे खोने का खयाल ही आंखों को नम कर जाता है।

Sudiksha kshatriya

Miss sudiksha Kshatriya is 16 years old and belongs to Bhopal Madhya Pradesh. She is currently studying in 12th grade. She has been passionate about writing since she was 8years old. An incident in her life inspired her to write poems. She loves writing. Besides writing, she is also a YouTuber .she also loves to feed and take care of street dogs.
Instagram id @sudikshakshatriya and @positive._.thoughts._.poem

DAD

since I was born you held my hand ,
after all you were my dad .

you taught me how to walk ,
so I can be besides you when you couldn't talk.

you taught me how to read and write ,
and made me eligible for the fight, of life .

you gave me my own personality ,
and individuality

you were with me through my good and bad,
after all you were my dad .

it was hard to see you leave me forever ,
and to think that we will be no longer together.

I didn't want to cry when I was saying bye,
cause i wanted it to be final happy goodbye .

cause you taught me to be bold and brave ,
and you gave me the power to watch your grave ,
after all you were my dad ,
after all you were my dad .

Saloni Gupta

Saloni is a rookie writer from Mumbai She is in
TyBcom. She has been writing her thoughts in
form of quotes since She was in 9th as her hobby.
She wants to be a Professor in future.

Insta id :- @thought_catalog7901

कुछ बातें तुम करे, कुछ हर्फ मैं कहूं
इस लफ़्ज़ों के खेल में,
मुझसे कभी तुम जीतो
और कभी मैं ख़ुद हार जाऊं!!

Silachi Kumar " Vयोgi "

Varanasi Student of M.A D.O.B : 24 January
Zodiac Sign : Aquarius Thoughtful, Artist, Nature,
Music and Animal Lover Humoristic and

Optimistic " आशावादी " Pen Name : Vयोgi Vयोgi

की कलम से (आपका #Vयोgi)

Insta id :- @silachie

" वो रातें "

HASTE ZAKHM

वो रातें कैसे भूल सकता हूँ..!
हाँ वही रातें, जब तुमसे पहली मुलाकात हुई थी,
फिर सारी रात जमकर, मन भर हमारी बात हुई थी ।
मानों जैसे छायी थी इश्क की बदरी
और जज़्बातों की बरसात हुई थी ।
हाँ..! आज भी वो रातें याद करता हूँ तो
चेहरे पर मुस्कान सी आ जाती है ।
फिर जब ध्यान आता है कि...
हमारी बाते अब ख़त्म हो चुकीं और
हमारे बीच अब कोई संबंध न रहा तो
सहसा, मेरी आँखें भर आती हैं ।
अगर आँखें बन्द कर सोना भी चाहूँ तो
नींद ही नहीं आती है...
क्योंकि, सारी रात मेरी पलकें यूँ भिगी रह जाती हैं ।

आपका #Vयोg

Do_lafz Ankit Chahal

Do_lafj 📖 📖 zindgi mast 😂 😂

HASTE ZAKHM

Zindagi ko kis mod par le jana h
Yeh khud ke upar h dost
Kyunki yaha log na raasta
Theek dikhate h na manzil..

Trapti Gupta

Trapti Gupta from Sakin, uttar pradesh. She is the daughter of Mr. Akhilesh Gupta and Mrs. Kalpna Gupta. She is studying in B.Sc (2nd year). Her hobbies are Drawing, painting, writing etc. Her Aim is to be an IAS officer nd also she wanted to achieve many more in this writing field which is her passion. She likes to decorate her feelings on a paper. She has participated in so many anthologies as a co-author with different publication and compiler of one anthology.

Insta id :- @heartposts__

HASTE ZAKHM

Her tears were
Sign of her
The broken pieces
Of her heart
She wanted to shed
each and every leaf
of his memories
like a tree does in autumn
She opened her wardrobe
to throw away
all those things which
makes her nostalgic
But she couldn't find
anything without his
memories
Suddenly she realized
that she is doing
like the Musk deer
which keeps on wandering
in search of the fragrance
She can't get rid of
his memories by discarding
her wardrobe
Because her whole existence
has absorbed the perfume
of his memories
and it is inseparable

PATHAN FATIMA B.Alam

Bio= this is a unique poem written by Pathan Fatima that will inspire you to bring your best in you . This poem is a journey of self discovery and enlightenment. The writeup are small and simple but their depth and impact is strong ♥ . This will not only become your guide in tough times in life and fight through adversities but also become a friend and bring a smile on your face in good times ♥ .

Insta id :- emaa_92x

HASTE ZAKHM

Hiding the hurt, hiding the pain,
Hiding the tears that fall like rain.
Saying I'm fine when I'm anything but.
This ache in my soul rips at my gut.
My skin is on fire; I burn from within.
The calm on my face is an ongoing sin.
The world must stay out; I've built up a wall.
My fragile lie will collapse should it ever fall.
Loneliness consumes me; it eats away the years
Until my life is swallowed by unending fears.
Waiting for someone to see I wear a mask
And care enough to remove it; is that too much to
ask?

Tannu Kumari

Hello everyone out there. This is me Tannu Kumari.
I am very passionate about writing. Hope u like my
writing. If you, then let me know through my
Instagram I'd. Thank you..
Insta id :- tannukumari198

HASTE ZAKHM

कभी तो दिखाओ
प्यार है तो दिखाओ न
गुस्सा हो तो बताओ न
दो पल के लिए ही सही
मुझे गले लगाओ न
जब नहीं समझती तुम्हे मैं
तो मुझे अच्छे से समझाओ न
ज्यादा तो नही मांगा तुमसे मैने
बस जब अकेली पड़ जाऊ
आकर मेरा सहारा बन जाओ न
कभी बिना वजह ही
मेरे पास आओ न
सच में प्यार है
तो कभी तो दिखाओ न।

Pankaj THAKUR

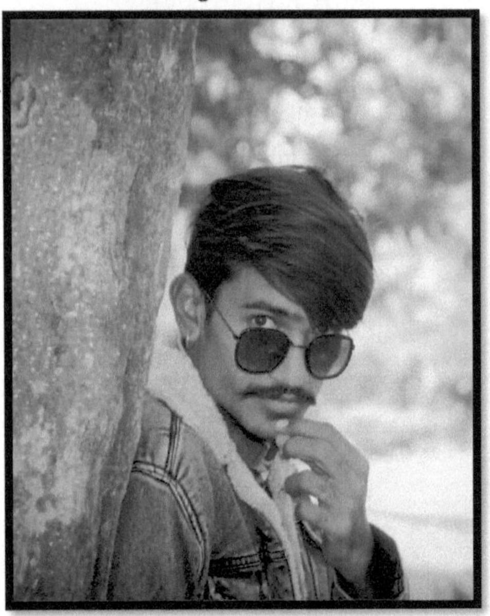

I am from Jaipur Rajasthan
I have been writing from 3 years
Mostly interested in writing poems and quotes. I
like to write and discuss about the topics related
to society and common people's daily life. I
always try to spread love and respect in one's
heart through my write-ups. For more information
and many more shayaris, quotes, poetries,
visit my Instagram I'd
@parmish_ke_ankahi_baatein__

HASTE ZAKHM

इज़हार-ए-इश्क

तमन्ना बहुत थी उन्हें हम से

आज उन तमन्नाओं को पूरा कोई ओर कर रहा है।।

उन्हें मालूम है हमें मोहब्बत है उनसे

वो इज़हार-ए-इश्क किसी ओर से बयां कर रहा हैं।।

जों ख्वाब हमने उनके साथ देखें

आज उन ख्वाब को हकीकत कोई ओर बना रहा है।।

जिस दिल में हम बसें थे

आज उस दिल में कोई ओर है उनके।।

हमारी मोहब्बत अब भी उनसे,

बस फर्क इतना है जो मोहब्बत हमारी थी वो मोहब्बत

अब किसी ओर की है।।

Abhishek mehra

@002abhi ✍☐♡

Insta id :- @aalfazzz_dilla_de

HASTE ZAKHM

(पहला प्यार)

जब देखा पहली बार उसे ,

उसके हाथ मैं किताब थी

वो सुनहरी रंग की जुल्फे उसकी

मुझे डसने के लिए बेताब थी

हर रोज मेरी गली मे से,

उसका आना जाना था

मेरा भी उसे देखने का ,

रोज नया बहाना था

याद है मुझे हमारी पहली मुलाकात

जब वो मुझसे टकराई थी

अपनी नीली आंखों को झुकाकर

धीरे से मुस्कुराई थी

उसकी बाते थी मजाक भरी

मेरी बातो मे इजहार था

भूल नही सकता उसको मैं

वो मेरा पहला पहला प्यार प्यार था

Disha gupta

This is disha. I m in 11nth standard from jabalpur. I love the swirl of words as they tangle human emotions

Insta id :- dishaxx5

HASTE ZAKHM

A mask

I smile, I laugh, I joke around,
but my feelings no one has ever found.
They see me every day with a smile on my
face,
but when I get back to this place
I feel as if it's my own hell,
as if I'm locked in a cell.
The tears run down my face.
I sit in my room, quiet and wondering
if anyone sees the pain I feel
and how it's oh so real.
Another day comes as I put on my mask and
hide.
No one sees the pain I feel inside.
I laugh and I smile,
but inside I'm sad.
I wish someone could see.
I get back to this place I call hell,
where it all began and where I fell.
I take off my mask, but I'm still all alone,
and it kills me that no one will ever know.
I wish I could be the girl
that people think they really see

-disha gupta

Adam JOSEPH Abram

Adam joseph abram is a prolific writer and philosopher.He is now twenty four years old. He has a degree in English language and literature from Mahatma University.Intellectual interventions have been made on various subjects. Now in the works of a new novel. Theoretical review through experience is the method.What he is trying to achieve is to innovate in the world of writing.

Insta id :- adam-joseph-abram

HASTE ZAKHM

Footsteps are distances Time also passes within walking distances If life's journeys are comfortable, so am I, Long distances to walk. What I discovered from the realization that life is fleeting was the fleetingness of my life.

This time will pass and life will continue It's just a continuation of something. The pleasures that last only moments and the sorrows that last ages. Absolutely nothing could be found in the loneliness.

I wanted to live a boring life, but it's going back to me, it's paving the way for me, I'm realizing that I have a long way to go. I wanted to walk thinking that winter would make me happy but on the same path but nothing.

Similarly I stood watching summer and spring and winter pass by on the same path yes tired. I have a lot of ways to run and hide only from myself can not run away. I'm tired of finding myself anywhere.

I still wish I could understand the meaning of this sentence if I could understand in life that there is truth in it. This time will also pass.

Kavya Mittal

"Turn your can't into can and dreams into plans!"
I am kavya mittal, a student of grade 10, just a
beginner in this writing world. I am looking
forward for being an motivational author &
speaker, trying to inspire others and a step
towards happy India!!

Insta id :- pen_vibes26

Life

Life has its ups and downs,
Just like waves.
Life has its twists and turns,
Just like maze.
Life is like a game,
Depending on how we play.
Life is like a game of poker,
Depending on how we are.
Life is like a tree Filled with leaves,
Life is like a space
Filled with undiscovered stars.
Life is like a money,
Loved and hated, abused and wanted.
Life has no definition,
But has a meaning.
Life has its ways,
Life has its days.
Everyone has their own reason and dreams to live
a life.

www.ingramcontent.com/pod-product-compliance
Lightning Source LLC
LaVergne TN
LVHW091109180726
843490LV00002B/689